THE PUBLIC LIBRARY
OF THE CITY OF BOSTON
BUILT BY THE PEOPLE
AND DEDICATED TO
THE ADVANCEMENT
OF LEARNING
AD MDCCCLXXXVIII

FREE TO ALL

A HANDBOOK TO THE ART AND ARCHITECTURE OF THE BOSTON PUBLIC LIBRARY

VISITORS GUIDE TO THE
MCKIM BUILDING · COPLEY SQUARE
ITS MURAL DECORATIONS AND
ITS COLLECTIONS

PREPARED BY PETER ARMS WICK
PHOTOGRAPHS BY RICHARD W. CHEEK
BOSTON · THE ASSOCIATES OF THE
BOSTON PUBLIC LIBRARY · 1977

Copyright © 1978 by The Associates
of the Boston Public Library

LCC Card No. 78-1445

ISBN 0-89073-054-7

Design by Lance Hidy

Typesetting by Michael & Winifred Bixler

Printing by The Meriden Gravure Co.

LIBRARY OF CONGRESS CATALOGING IN PUBLICATION DATA

Wick, Peter A.
  A handbook to the art and architecture of the Boston Public Library.

  Bibliography: p.
  1. Boston. Public Library. 2. Library architecture—Massachusetts—Boston. 3. Art—Massachusetts—Boston. I. Title.
Z733.B75H35   917.44'61   78-1445
ISBN 0-89073-054-7

INTRODUCTION

This is a handbook to the art and architecture of the Boston Public Library. A library is not just a building, but a building does stand for its library, and the Boston Public Library at Copley Square is not only a treasure house of millions of books, manuscripts, music scores, prints, etc. but the building itself is a thing of great beauty and significance. Built by and for the people some eighty-two years ago, this McKim, Mead and White designed building has long been hailed as an exemplary public monument, a work of art. Since 1973 it has been officially designated a National Historic Landmark.

For generations, visitors from near and far have come to admire the elegance of the architecture and the beauty of its decoration: the murals, the sculptures, and its cloistered courtyard, a quiet oasis in the middle of a bustling city. But the splendor of the marble and the glory of the murals speak not only for the cosmopolitan taste and generous spirit of a people a century ago, but perhaps more importantly, they bear witness to the dedication and trust of a citizenry who believed in the raison d'être of the public library, that it was "built by the people and dedicated to the advancement of learning."

The Library is today still blessed with friends who believe in the support of their public library. Among them are the Associates of the Boston Public Library who share their love for and pride in this institution and what it stands for. With gifts of money, collections, and just as importantly, their time and talents, these friends keep up the age-old Boston tradition in their reverence for

learning, appreciation of art, and their desire and willingness to share these with others. This handbook is an anniversary gift from the Associates on the occasion of the Library's 125th Birthday. The Library is grateful to its many friends whose support makes this publication possible, and particularly to the officers of the Associates: Bruce Beal, Frances Howe and Charlotte Vershbow, as well as to Peter Wick, who generously devoted much time and shared his incomparable knowledge and insight in preparing this booklet for us, so that friends old and new will be able to discover (or rediscover) and enjoy this many-splendored building and all it has to offer.
Yen-Tsai Feng

FOREWORD

This handbook of the Boston Public Library on Copley Square, which opened its doors to the public in February 1895, serves as a visitor's pocket guide to the masterpiece of the architect Charles Follen McKim, with a brief description of the architecture and artistic embellishment of the McKim Building, and a selection of those works of art currently on view. The last comparable handbook was written in 1921, and last reprinted in 1939. The first handbook appeared in 1895, with fullsome descriptions of every detail of the building and especially the mural decoration. Perhaps on the occasion of the 125th Anniversary of the founding of the Boston Public Library, this simplified handbook with its photographs by Richard W. Cheek will serve in some small degree to recreate the fervor, genius and creative energy that went into the epic of its building.

P. A. W.

PHOTOGRAPHS

BY RICHARD W. CHEEK

1. The Boston Public Library, Exterior View
2. The 1972 addition to the Library designed by Philip Johnson
3. Detail of the Cornice
4. Detail of the Entrance Gates, Copley Square
5. Relief of the Library Seal by Augustus Saint-Gaudens
6. Minerva, Keystone of Central Arch by Domingo Mora
7. Vestibule with MacMonnies' statue of Sir Harry Vane
8. Bronze Doors by Daniel Chester French
    a. Music and Poetry (left)
    b. Knowledge and Wisdom (center)
    c. Truth and Romance (right)
9. Main Entrance Hall
10. Mosaic Vaulting in Main Entrance Hall
11. Colonnade of Interior Court
12. Interior Court
13. Memorial Lion by Louis Saint-Gaudens
14. Main Staircase from Landing
15. Second Floor Loggia with *Muses* by Puvis de Chavannes
16. Second Floor Loggia
17. Overdoor of Venetian Lobby with 16th century Stone Relief of Lion of St. Mark and mural supporters by Joseph Lindon Smith
18. Bates Hall
19. Detail of Entrance Vestibule to Bates Hall
20. Trustees Room
21. French Renaissance Mantelpiece, white limestone with carved arabesques, Trustees Room
22. Detail of Italian Renaissance Mantelpiece, white Sienna marble, Cheverus Room (formerly Treasure Room)
23. Government Documents Room (formerly Periodical Room)
24. Detail of Ceiling Decoration, *The Triumph of Time*, by John Elliot (1858–1925) painted in artist's studio in Rome, unveiled March, 1901 in Elliot Room (formerly the Teachers' Reference Room)
25. Delivery Room with Edwin Austin Abbey Murals, *The Quest of the Holy Grail*

26. Edwin Austin Abbey, Round Table with fable of the Seat Perilous, from mural series of *The Quest of the Holy Grail*
27. Delivery Room Mantelpiece with Abbey Mural, *The Castle of the Maidens*
28. Sargent Hall looking towards north end, showing Hebraic portion of murals by John Singer Sargent, R.A. Sargent designed and decorated entire hall including architectural enframement, the overdoor relief of dolphins, the pictures frames, medallions, and lighting fixtures
29. John Singer Sargent Mural at south end showing Christian Portion with the Trinity, the Dogma of the Redemption and the relief Crucifixus
30. Sargent Panel, *The Synagogue*, over staircase
31. Sargent Panel, *The Church*, over staircase
32. Detail of Sargent's *Frieze of the Prophets* with Hosea in white cloak
33. Sargent Panel, *Our Lady of Sorrows*, on the west wall
34. John Singleton Copley, *Charles I Demanding in the House of Commons the Five Impeached Members*, oil painting, 1782–1795, in Cheverus Room (formerly Treasure Room)
35. Portrait of Joshua Bates, copy by Eden Upton Eddis (1812–1901), English painter, of his original oil
36. Portrait of Benjamin Franklin by Joseph-Siffred Duplessis (1725–1802), in Cheverus Room
37. Hiram Powers (1805–1873), bust of Jared Sparks (1789–1866), replica of the original executed in Florence in 1859, in Memorial Hall, Cambridge
38. Martin Millmore (1849–1883), bust of George Ticknor, (1791–1871)
39. Thomas Ball (1819–1911), bust of Edward Everett (1794–1865), 1864
40. Capt. Francis Derwent Wood, R.A., (1872–1926), bust of Henry James (1843–1916), 1914
41. Horatio Greenough (1805–1852), bust of Christ
42. Leopoldo Ansiglione (Italy, 1832–1899), Marble of Child and Swan
43. Antonio Canova (1757–1822), marble copy after, of Venus, a pendant to the copy of the Venus de Medici
44. William Wetmore Story (1819–1895), Arcadian Shepherd Boy, 1855

1. The Boston Public Library, designed by Charles F. McKim

THE BOSTON PUBLIC LIBRARY

THE INSTITUTION

Above the helmeted head of Minerva on the keystone of the central arch of the Boston Public Library cut in bold raised granite letters is the simple statement FREE·TO·ALL. This is not the empty rhetoric of a proud citizenry, but the ringing truth. Dr. Oliver Wendell Holmes had struck the note in his declamatory poem at the corner-stone laying in Copley Square on 28 September 1888:

> Let in the light! from every age
> Some gleams of garnered wisdom pour,

And in another stanza:

> Behind the ever-open gate
> No pikes shall fence a crumbling throne
> No lackeys cringe, no courtiers wait,—
> This palace is the people's own!

Founded in 1852, first opened to the public in 1854, the Boston Public Library is the pioneer of free municipal libraries in any American city supported by general taxation. Its collecting, circulating and lending policies are based on far-sighted principles of public education conceived by such founding trustees as George Ticknor and Edward Everett, supported by such enlightened city administrators as Mayors Josiah Quincy, Jr. and John Prescott Bigelow, and developed by such early Librarians as Charles Coffin Jewett and Justin Winsor. It received its first large gift from Joshua Bates, a London banker in the firm of Baring Brothers who started life as a poor, book-hungry boy in Weymouth, Massachusetts. The first library

2. The 1972 addition to the Library designed by Philip Johnson

building in Boylston Street, on the site now occupied by the Colonial Theatre, was opened in 1858 with a collection of seventy thousand volumes. In 1895, with an expansion to six hundred and ten thousand books, it was removed to its present location in Copley Square.

In 1972 a new addition, designed by the New York architect Philip Johnson, opened its doors, its main entrance facade filling out the city block on Boylston Street. This spacious, elegant building, fully consistent with the artistic and operational demands of modern Boston, joined with the McKim building on Copley Square to form the Central Library comprising an expanded General Library of some 750,000 volumes on open shelves with a seating capacity of 1200, and a Research Library headquartered in the McKim building, with its more than 3,000,000 volumes of printed books, maps, documents, newspapers, microtexts, recordings, prints, and manuscripts.

The Library is supported by public funds from the City of Boston, with income from endowments used for acquisition of special library materials. It also serves as the headquarters library of the Eastern Massachusetts Regional Library System, with additional support from the Commonwealth of Massachusetts. The control of the Library is vested in an unpaid board of five Trustees, appointed by the Mayor.

THE McKIM BUILDING

One of Boston's proudest monuments, perhaps the most admired, discussed and influential public building in the American architectural evolution of the nineteenth century, the Boston Public Library, facing historic Copley Square, marks the supreme achievement of its architect, Charles F. McKim, senoir partner in the New York firm of McKim, Mead & White. The challenge to McKim was complex: to erect a civic building of commanding presence in juxtaposition to, yet not overpowering, the picturesque Richardsonian Romanesque of Trinity Church, the masterpiece of the Eighties. The solution was brilliant, resulting in the first outstanding example of Renaissance Beaux Arts academicism in the United States, which set a new standard of scholarly taste and elegance. Serene classical horizontality and smooth white sparkling granite contrasted with the soaring irregular mass and rough-hewn ashlar of Trinity. The models for McKim's famed facade are three: Labrouste's Bibliothèque Sainte-Geneviève in Paris, Alberti's Tempio Malatestiano in Rimini, and Richardson's Marshall Field Wholesale Store in Chicago. But the Library's elevation gained its own noble aesthetic, not through exterior expression of interior function, but through its proportion and clarity, and the chiseled precision of its details. Few buildings to this day in America have inspired such nobility of spirit nor surpassed the structural perfection of its stone cutting.*

THE EXTERIOR

The exterior elevation facing Copley Square is 225 feet long and 70 feet high from sidewalk to cornice. The building is set on a broad granite platform raising it above the flatness of the square. It follows the general divisions of a Renaissance *palazzo* with a heavy lower story, in effect a high rusticated basement, supporting an upper story with smoother joints pierced by thirteen lofty window arches, which with the three central entrance arches below, counterbalance the strong horizontal lines of string courses, frieze, crowning copper cornice and cresting atop the red-tiled roof. The Milford granite blocks are grayish-white reflecting faint pinkish lights. A bold inscription cut in Roman capitals just below the cornice reads:

* Royal Cortissoz wrote that to McKim "building materials were what pigments are to the painter; he handled them with the same intensely personal feeling for their essential qualities that a great technician of the brush brings to the manipulation of his colors, and he left upon his productions the same autographic stamp."

 The Boston Public Library was built by Woodbury & Leighton, the Boston contractors. The brickwork of the Interior Court was carried out by Norcross Brothers, the Worcester contractors who had built Trinity Church for H. H. Richardson.

THE PUBLIC LIBRARY OF THE CITY OF
BOSTON BUILT BY THE PEOPLE AND DEDICATED
TO THE ADVANCEMENT OF LEARNING.
A.D. MDCCCLXXXVIII.

The Boylston Street inscription reads:

THE COMMONWEALTH REQUIRES THE
EDUCATION OF THE PEOPLE AS THE
SAFEGUARD OF ORDER AND LIBERTY.

The frieze on the Blagden Street side is inscribed:

MDCCCLII. FOUNDED THROUGH THE MUNIFICENCE
AND PUBLIC SPIRIT OF CITIZENS.

Above the frieze at the roofline is a noble cornice crowning the façade. The upper portion of the cornice is ornamented with a row of lions' heads, the whole topped by an elaborate green copper cresting, the motif of which, as in the seals over the entrance, is the regularly recurring dolphin, symbol of Boston's maritime status. The skyline of the pantiled roof is enriched with a second copper cresting, and terminating at the corners of the building in handsome metal masts.

3. Detail of the Cornice

EXTERIOR DETAILS

On the platform flanking the front entrance of the Library, set into massive granite pedestals, are two heroic seated female figures in bronze (dated 1911), the work of the Boston sculptor Bela L. Pratt: that on the right personifying *Art*, and on the left *Science* with names of the world's most eminent artists and scientists carved on the granite blocks. Originally, these two groups had been assigned pride of place to the sculptor Augustus Saint-Gaudens who had played a formative role in advising McKim on the embellishment of the Library, and propounded the concept of an American Renaissance collaborative of the ablest architects, painters, and sculptors achieving a harmony of the arts in an edifice proclaiming native pride and the public elevation of taste.*

The soffits of the three entrance arches are carved with a double row of deep rosetted caissons or panels. On the keystone of the center arch is sculpted the helmeted head of Minerva, goddess of wisdom, the work of Saint-Gaudens and Domingo Mora. Each arch is enclosed with heavy wrought-iron gates and set off by the four clusters of large branched candelabra which provide a dark and sweeping thrust against the flat masonry profile. Above, under the great central windows are three seals of the Commonwealth, of the Library and of the City of Boston, carved in relief in pink Knoxville marble. The central seal was carved by Saint-Gaudens as adapted from a design for the library device by Kenyon Cox. It portrays two nude boys holding torches, acting as supporters to a shield

---

* By May 1899 Saint-Gaudens had made working models: on one pedestal *Labor*, representing a man seated between two female figures of *Science* and *Art*; on the other, a male figure of *Law* between figures of *Power* and *Religion*. Delays and ultimately death thwarted the completion of his commission. One notes on the existing pedestals the classical device of the laurel wreath, a concept of Saint-Gaudens used throughout the Library, and carrying through the sculptor's own work and supervisory role, as in the Unknown Soldier's Tomb in Arlington Cemetery.

4. Detail of the Entrance Gates, Copley Square

5. Relief of the Library Seal by Augustus Saint-Gaudens

6. Minerva, Keystone of Central Arch by Domingo Mora

which bears an open book and the dates of founding and incorporation of the Library. Above is the motto *Omnium lux Civium* ("The Light of all Citizens"), while in the background are dolphins and laurel branches. The thirty-three granite medallions in the spandrels of the window arches on the three façades contain the trade devices of early printers carved by Mora.

THE VESTIBULE

The floors, walls and vaulted ceiling are of pink Knoxville marble; the floor is inlaid with patterns of brown Knoxville and Levanto marble. The three doorways leading to the Main Entrance Hall are copied from the entrance to the Temple of Erectheus on the Acropolis of Athens.

The bronze statue in the deep niche on the left as one enters the vestibule is by Frederick MacMonnies. The richly dressed, dashing cavalier is a representation of Sir Harry Vane, youthful Governor of Massachusetts Bay Colony in 1636 and 1637. An aristocrat, but also a Puritan, he was beheaded in 1662, in England, for rebellion against the King.*

The six bronze doors, each weighing fifteen hundred pounds apiece, are the work of the sculptor Daniel Chester French with allegorical figures arranged in pairs: *Music* and *Poetry* (left), *Knowledge* and *Wisdom* (center), and *Truth* and *Romance* (right).* In their day, this decorative abandonment of the broad surface of metal to draped human figures, about six feet high, carried relief sculpture into an advanced realm by their lack of enframement or pannelling, and by their shallow relief which never exceeded 1⅜ inches. The figures, holding aloft their attributes, with rhythmic folds of drapery, combine American idealism with the elegance of the Second Empire tradition.

THE MAIN ENTRANCE HALL

This low hall, divided into three aisles by heavy pieces of Iowa sandstone, is of Roman design. The mosaic ceiling, arched in the center aisle and with vaulted domes in the side bays, is decorated with a vine-covered trellis and inscribed with the

* The statue was presented to the Library by Dr. Charles G. Weld in honor of James Freeman Clark, D. D., an eminent Unitarian minister who was, at the time of his death, a Trustee of the Library.

* The superb castings are by the John Williams Foundry, and were installed by January 1905.

7. Vestibule with MacMonnies' statue of Sir Harry Vane

8. Bronze Doors by Daniel Chester French
   a. Music and Poetry

8b. Knowledge and Wisdom

8c. Truth and Romance

names of six illustrious Bostonians: Pierce, Adams, Franklin, Emerson, Hawthorne, and Longfellow. In the pendentives of the domes are the names of twenty-four more Boston worthies—the theologians, Channing, Parker, Mather, and Eliot; the reformers, Sumner, Phillips, Mann, and Garrison; the scientists, Gray, Agassiz, Rumford, and Bowditch; the artists, Allston, Copley, Stuart, and Bulfinch; the historians, Parkman, Motley, Bancroft, and Prescott; the jurists, Webster, Choate, Shaw, and Story.

The floor is of white Georgia marble, inlaid in the center aisle with brass intarsia representing the symbols and signs of the zodiac, an inscription commemorating the founding of the Library (1852) and the beginning of the construction of the Copley Square building (1888), the Library seal, and a laurel wreath with the names of eight men prominently connected with the establishment and early history of the Library. They include three early trustees, Edward Everett, John Prescott Bigelow (who was earlier Mayor of Boston), and George Ticknor; Josiah Quincy, Jr., Mayor of Boston; Joshua Bates and

9. Main Entrance Hall

10. Mosaic Vaulting in Main Entrance Hall

11. Colonnade of Interior Court

Robert C. Winthrop, early benefactors; Charles Coffin Jewett, the institution's first great librarian (1858–1868); and Alexander Vattemare, the ubiquitous Frenchman whose zeal for the international exchange of books helped to stir the ferment that led to the founding of the Library.

THE INTERIOR COURT

Main access to the Interior Court is from the two side corridors off the Entrance Hall. One steps onto an arcaded promenade of white marble framing three sides of a rectangular green parterre and reflecting pool, in its perfect proportions a near copy of the arcade of the first story of the Palazzo della Cancelleria in Rome. The marble of the arches, cornice and parapet comes from Georgia; once pure white, it is slowly turning pale gold; the marble of the columns comes from Tuckahoe, New York, today a soft gray-white. The floor of the arcade is set off in a herringbone pattern of red brick banded with marble. The ceiling is vaulted in plaster, while the inner walls are of granite sparsely pierced by two tiers of windows, the lower tier covered with iron grilles. The upper walls of the courtyard are of yellowish-gray brick of a long thin module, skillfully laid, with trim of Milford granite.

In the granite walls of the arcade are four memorials in bronze: a bust of General Francis A. Walker, once a Trustee of the Library, by Richard E. Brooks; a medallion portrait of Robert C. Billings, one of the Library's benefactors, by Augustus Saint-Gaudens; a tablet in memory of Thomas Sergeant Perry, who "enriched this Library by his wise counsel and his rare learning during half a century"; and a tablet to commemorate the employees of the Library who served in World War I.

THE MAIN STAIRCASE

From the Entrance Hall opens the Main Staircase which struck Henry James for "its amplitude of wing and its splendour of tawny marble, a high and luxurious beauty." The walls are sheathed in variegated yellow Sienna marble veined in black, which was specially quarried for the Library. With the sunlight pouring in from the three high arched windows above the landing looking on the Court, the glowing color effect of yellow, saffron, topaz and amber blend in a surface of indescribable richness. The steps are of ivory-gray French échaillon mar-

12. Interior Court

13. Memorial Lion by Louis Saint-Gaudens

ble, mottled with fossil shells. The deeply coffered ceiling is of plaster, cream colored and light blue; from it hangs a spherical chandelier of bronze and cut glass.

The floor of the landing is inlaid with hexagonal and diamond-shaped patterns of red-streaked Numidian marble from Africa. Centered on the landing are heavy oak doors with carved panels leading out to a balcony overlooking the Interior Court. Guarding the landing at the turn of the stairs are the two regal couchant lions carved from solid blocks of unpolished Sienna marble, the work of Louis Saint-Gaudens, brother of Augustus; each is a memorial to the men of the two Massachusetts Volunteer Infantry regiments who fell in the Civil War. Lettered in bronze on the pedestals are the names of battles and campaigns in which the regiments participated.

14. Main Staircase from Landing

THE PUVIS DE CHAVANNES MURALS

On mounting the upper flight of the Main staircase from the landing, one is arrested by the painted wall decorations by Puvis de Chavannes (1824–1898), the cycle of Arcadian allegories commissioned by the Library from France's greatest master of mural decoration, which though executed in his seventy-second year, showed no failing power in perfecting this difficult assignment, fresh as he was from the triumphant success of his murals in the Hôtel de Ville in Paris. As seen through the five-arched loggia of McKim's second floor corridor, a vestibule to the Main Reading Room, these serene decorations are in complete classical harmony with their architectural setting. The main panel *Les Muses Inspiratrices Acclament Le Génie, Mes-*

15. Second Floor Loggia with *Muses* by Puvis de Chavannes

sager de Lumière ("The Muses of Inspiration welcoming the Spirit of Light"), like all the Library murals is painted on canvas affixed to the wall, and is approximately 20 feet high by 40 feet long. It represents the nine Muses of Greek mythology flying upward from the olive and laurel groves of the Hill of Parnassus to acclaim the nude youth representing the Spirit of Enlightenment. The aerial quality and poetic ambience of these silvery white-clad figures set against the pale tones of green earth, blue water and ethereal sky, uplifts the imagination with a breadth and grandeur that sets the aspirational theme of the Library's programme.

The eight smaller panels in the upper arches of the staircase wall represent the main disciplines of poetry, philosophy and science, said to conform rationally to the Library's catalogue classifications: on the right, Pastoral, Dramatic and Epic Poetry; on the left, History, Astronomy and Philosophy; on the wall to left and to right of the window, Chemistry and Physics.*

The floor of the Chavannes Gallery (recently replaced in close conformity with the original specifications) is a pattern of yellow Verona, gray Bottichino, dark gray Aldorado and reddish gray Chiampo Perlato marbles.

---

* "It was a happy and liberal thought," as Fenollosa said, "to call to this our first American Pantheon, a master of that old world in which ours had root."

The last of the panels was installed in October 1896: The *Muses* canvas is signed *P. Puvis de Chavannes 95*; *Epic Poetry* is signed *P. Puvis de Chavannes Paris 1896*.

The contract signed by the Trustees and artist was dated July 7, 1893. The artist's fee was 250,000 francs ($50,000) paid in installments from 1893 to 1896 from City appropriations for the building and its decoration.

In a letter to Sargent dated 19 December 1896, McKim wrote: "The Chavannes work is superb in its stately proportions and high ideals, carried out with a breadth that easily makes him a master of his art. The public have hailed it by common acclaim. He has made it his staircase rather than that of McKim, Meade & White, and I am sure that it cannot fail to deeply impress you."

16. Second Floor Loggia

BATES HALL

Bates Hall, named after the first great benefactor of the Library, serves as the Main Reading Room, and is entered through the central door off the Staircase Corridor (Puvis de Chavannes loggia). Even by today's standards one is impressed by the majestic scale of this Roman hall (218 feet long × 42½ feet wide × 50 feet high) with its rich barrel vault running the full length of the Copley Square façade and lighted by fifteen arched and grilled windows. The ends of the Hall are enclosed by vaulted half-domes. The sandstone used in the walls is from Amherst, Ohio; the floor is terrazzo bordered by yellow Verona marble; the Hall is surrounded by bookcases of

17. Overdoor of Venetian Lobby with 16th century Stone Relief of Lion of St. Mark and mural supporters by Joseph Lindon Smith

18. Bates Hall

English oak standing about ten feet high,* erected on a base of red Verona marble, and set off by a pantheon of white marble busts representing great authors and eminent Bostonians; in the high frieze carved in gilt letters are the names of the world's most illustrious thinkers and artists. Over the central doorway is a richly carved balcony of Indiana limestone, while

* The carpentry work in the Public Library was done by Ira G. Hersey, whose factory was in Cambridgeport. It included the wainscoting of the Delivery Room, the panelled oak doors throughout the building, the wainscot at the south end of Bates Hall, and the miles of shelving.

The firm of Mellish, Byfield & Co. of Boston received the contract for the furniture, consisting of tables, catalog cases, newspaper and periodical stands, desks, chairs, etc.; also the oak screens at either end of Bates Hall.

19. Detail of Entrance Vestibule to Bates Hall

20. Trustees Room

the ornate doors at the ends of the Hall on the same inner wall are carved of black Belgian and Alps green serpentine marble with columns crowned by bronze Corinthian capitals; in the adjoining bays are two Renaissance mantels of sandstone and red Verona marble.

McKim and Saint-Gaudens had selected Whistler to paint the enframed panel at the Boylston Street end of the Hall but negotiations progressed so badly that the contract was withdrawn. The commission was then offered to John LaFarge but his scheme likewise failed to materialize and the ill-fated mural remains blank to this day.

21. French Renaissance Mantelpiece, white limestone with carved arabesques, Trustees Room

22. Detail of Italian Renaissance Mantelpiece, white Sienna marble Cheverus Room (formerly Treasure Room)

23. Government Documents Room (formerly Periodical Room)

24. Detail of Ceiling Decoration, *The Triumph of Time*, by John Elliot (1858–1925) painted in artist's studio in Rome, unveiled March, 1901 in Elliot Room (formerly the Teachers' Reference Room)

THE DELIVERY ROOM

From the Puvis de Chavannes Vestibule one passes to the right through the small red Pompeian Lobby into the somber richness of the Delivery Room where the circulation desk for the Research Library is situated. Here the treatment is based on Venetian models of the Early Renaissance with a high wainscot paneling of oak, the heavily beamed ceiling decorated in the manner of the library of the Doge's Palace in Venice, the doorways and fireplace mantel with massive projecting entablatures and flanking Corinthian pilasters in a blood red *rouge antique* marble (the columns in green and red Levanto).* In the middle of the highly polished fireplace lintel is a laurel wreath carved in delicate relief with flying streamers containing the date MDCCCLII (1852), that of the founding of the Library. The floor is laid in contrasting squares of gray Istrian and red Verona marble.

The eight foot frieze between the wainscot and the ceiling is occupied by the Arthurian cycle of murals called the *Quest of the Holy Grail*, painted by the American artist resident in England, Edwin Austin Abbey, R. A. It was Abbey who designed the room as a setting for his colorful medieval romances drawn from episodes of the life of Sir Galahad and the knights of the Round Table based principally on Tennyson's "Idylls of the King." Here is a pictorial realism which has raised the genre of narrative illustration to a monumental scale of brilliant and dramatic pageantry, reflecting the high level of Pre-Raphaelite painting in England, and spurring the young man's fancy to chivalrous achievement.

---

* All the marble work in the Boston Public Library with the exception of that in the Grand Staircase was done by Bowker, Torrey & Co., Chardon Street, Boston. All the shaping and carving of the marble were done in the workrooms of the firm. The same firm executed the richly-carved balcony of Indiana limestone in Bates Hall, and the floor, wainscot and balustrades of Yorkshire and Amherst sandstone in Sargent Hall.

25. Delivery Room with Edwin Austin Abbey Murals, *The Quest of the Holy Grail*

26. Edwin Austin Abbey, Round Table with fable of the Seat Perilous, from mural series of *The Quest of the Holy Grail*

27. Delivery Room Mantlepiece with Abbey Mural, *The Castle of the Maidens*

The large central panel (No. 111) over the book delivery desk represents the Round Table and the curious fable of the "Seat Perilous" in which no man has yet sat with safety. The young Sir Galahad, knighted by Arthur, has sworn a vow to be worthy to take his place with the Companions of the Order seated in Arthur's hall. Sir Galahad, robed in red, is led by Joseph of Arimathea, an old man cloaked in white. King Arthur rises with bowed head from his canopied throne, while the knights raise the cross-shaped hilts of their swords in salute to the challenger. Overhead hovers a seraphic host of angels. Throughout the cycle Sir Galahad is clothed in red, symbolic of purity and enabling the spectator to readily identify the protagonist. In the process of installation, Abbey felt it necessary to build up his gilded halos in plastic relief to give sharper definition and enrichment to his design, a technique recommended by Sargent.*

In 1896, soon after the opening of the Library, Ernest Fenollosa wrote: "The significance of the mural painting in the Boston Public Library should now be plain. Here we have established the first great centre of a future civic series. Here the principle is first openly, and on a large scale, acknowledged by the public authorities. By their act, and by this first blaze of achievement, we set Boston as the earliest of the seats of public pilgrimage, *the veritable Assisi of American art*."

---

* Writing to Alma Tadema from New York on May 18, 1895 Abbey says: "We had a great time in Boston. I wish you could see the things in place—John's [Sargent's] looks stunning. You see it from a great distance below, and he has gilded the whole interior of the space and it is all lighted by a strong reflected light; it gains tremendously and as a conception is for the first time complete. We both suffered, as I have said, fearfully from the heat, working on scaffolds under the ceiling—I in a room crowded all day with people breathing hard. I think my affair looks better than it ever did before—although it has masses of detail which tell as nothing. I am pleased that it looks right in scale. I have learned a great deal seeing it in place and shall do the rest of it with greater confidence. Masses of tones tell, not detail, nor light and shade . . ."

THE SARGENT GALLERY

At the north end of the Puvis de Chavannes loggia one ascends to the upper floor of the Library by an enclosed stairway of gray sandstone adorned only by handrails of Alps green marble.* From the landing halfway up, a door opens on the balcony overlooking Bates Hall. One emerges on a dimly-lit vaulted corridor off which one enters the Albert H. Wiggin Gallery of Prints and Drawings, the Cheverus Room housing the Joan of Arc Collection donated by John Cardinal Wright, and the Charlotte Cushman Room. This long narrow hall, its height greater than its width, was specially reserved for the mural decorations of John Singer Sargent, R. A., who devoted thirty years of thought and labor in the execution of the sequence of panels on *Judaism* and *Christianity*, and himself designed the somber churchly setting in sandstone with its gilded architectural enframement. One must be aware that Sargent looked upon his mural decorations as the supreme achievement of his career, transcending his portraiture, and fulfilling the ultimate expression of his life-work. The work as it stands was placed in position in four installments: the paintings at the north end of the hall in 1895, the south end wall in 1903, the niches and vaulting at the south end and the lunettes along the side wall in 1916, and the two panels over the staircase in 1919.

---

* At the foot of the steps is a memorial tablet set into the wall, dedicated on March 3, 1931 by the Boston Society of the American Institute of Architects:

CHARLES FOLLEN McKIM

1847   ARCHITECT   1909

FAITHFUL SERVANT OF THE ARTS
INCOMPARABLE FRIEND TO YOUTH
HONOURED MASTER OF THE PROFESSION
IN THIS BUILDING ENDURINGLY IS REVEALED
THE SPLENDID AMPLITUDE OF HIS GENIUS
AN INSPIRATION TO ALL MEN

The unveiling of Sargent's pagan series on the north wall, representing the Children of Israel beneath the yoke of their oppressors, left a startling impression of modernity, with their

28. Sargent Hall looking towards north end, showing Hebraic portion of murals by John Singer Sargent, R.A. Sargent designed and decorated entire hall including architectural enframement, the overdoor relief of dolphins, the pictures frames, medallions, and lighting fixtures

blend of Egyptian and Assyrian styles combined with gilded Byzantine casts applied in relief to the surface. The haunting intensity and *terribilità* of the Pharoah against a grayish-blue and flaming ground, and the Assyrian monarch standing in regal splendor, with the Phoenician seductress Astarte on the ceiling vault, had never been seen on a wall before.

Less complex and decoratively elaborate is the Frieze of the Prophets below the symbolically-charged lunette. The plastic realm of these heroic figures in classic gestures and poses made them readily comprehensible within the human scheme of things. The central figure is Moses holding the tablets brought down from Sinai. Sargent had devoted thirty years to their study and execution using a succession of models and sketches in charcoal and oil plotting the drapery. He had induced Coventry Patmore to pose for Ezekiel, the dominant figure in a white hooded cloak in the group to the left of Moses. He also engaged Angelo Colarossi, the leading London model whom he shared with Abbey.*

The opposite south end of the hall, not completed until 1903, sets forth the Christian message of the Dogma of the Redemption. The powerful gilded Crucifixus modelled in bold relief is the binding motif combining the upper lunette showing the enthroned Persons of the Blessed Trinity with the Frieze of Angels below. A great red cope envelops the Trinity hemmed with a gold orphrey inscribed with *Sanctus* running repetitively through the composition like a ribbon. On the cornice that separates the frieze from the lunette is the Latin inscription taken from the Cathedral of Cefalù, Sicily (A.D. 1148): *Factus Homo, Factor Hominis, Factique Redemptor. Corporeus Redimo Corpora Corda Deus*". ("I, God in the flesh, man's maker and redeemer, Myself made man, redeem both body and soul.")

On the west wall *Our Lady of Sorrows* is represented as a

---

* Other models included Sargent's assistant Andrew O'Connor, Nicola d'Iverna and a succession of Italian models, and George Roller as Hosea, Nahum and Isaiah.

29. John Singer Sargent Mural at south end showing Christian Portion with the Trinity, the Dogma of the Redemption and the relief Crucifixus

votive figure above an altar behind a screen of lighted candles. The Virgin, which has an elaborate silver crown and halo, and is vested in a cope, stiff with embroidery, stands upon the crescent moon. The seven swords thrust into the heart of the Virgin typify the Seven Sorrows.

The two panels *Church* and *Synagogue* in architectural frames on the opposite wall over the staircase were finally installed in 1919 to complete Sargent's cycle. The Hebrew faith, which the

30–31. Sargent Panels, *The Synagogue* (left), and *The Church* (right), over staircase

32. Detail of Sargent's *Frieze of the Prophets* with Hosea in white cloak

33. Sargent Panel, *Our Lady of Sorrows*, on the west wall

artist has sympathetically shown as the great forerunner of Christianity was regarded by medieval churchmen as having forfeited its high place through its failure to recognize the claim of Christ as the expected Messiah, and was accordingly represented as blind and dethroned; the Church itself was naturally depicted as having succeeded to both the vision and the leadership lost by the Jewish religion. This view was expressed in the art of the Middle Ages by the opposition of two figures, the Synagogue, sightless and fallen; the Church, outlooking and triumphant.

CHRONOLOGY OF SARGENT MURALS
FOR BOSTON PUBLIC LIBRARY

January 18, 1893 First Contract. Sargent was paid $15,000 for decoration of north and south end walls.

1892–1894 North Wall lunette and ceiling painted on canvas in Edwin Abbey's studio at Fairford, Gloucestershire, and then exhibited at the Royal Academy, London.

April 25, 1895 Unveiling Pagan End in Boston Public Library. The lunette, ceiling and frieze were transported to Boston and installed. The canvas was tacked to the edge of the relevant wall space and firmly stuck to the wall with a solution of white lead.

December 5, 1895 Second Contract. Sargent was to be paid an additional $15,000 to be raised by subscription for the wall panels to join the two ends.

February 1903 Unveiling Medieval End

December 21, 1916 Unveiling Medieval Ceiling

October 5, 1919 Unveiling "Synagogue" and "Church" over staircase.

In a copy of a letter in the Boston Athenaeum written from 31 Tite Street, Chelsea, London, October 8, 1915, Sargent wrote to Josiah H. Benton, president of the Library trustees, describing various problems of decorating the upper landing. The last paragraph reads:

> ..."I have tried to make a good selection of Renaissance ornament throughout and not to do anything that would irritate the ghost of McKim. With the exception of some hints and warnings from a Belgian refugee, an architect of the name of Adrien Blomme, I have not consulted any architects, as I felt that Messrs. Fox & Gale were the only ones that I ought to consult. So I hope they will give me the benefit of their advice and criticism, or suggest a better scheme if mine will not work."

(Thomas A. Fox collaborated with Sargent in several of his mural projects. Fox's papers are in the Boston Athenaeum.)

34. John Singleton Copley, *Charles I Demanding in the House of Commons the Five Impeached Members*, oil painting, 1782–1795, in Cheverus Room (formerly Treasure Room)

35. Portrait of Joshua Bates, copy by Eden Upton Eddis (1812–1901), English painter, of his original oil

36. Portrait of Benjamin Franklin by Joseph-Siffred Duplessis (1725–1802), in Cheverus Room

37. Hiram Powers (1805–1873), bust of Jared Sparks (1789–1866), replica of the original

38. Martin Millmore (1849–1883), bust of George Ticknor, 1791–1871

39. Thomas Ball (1819–1911), bust of Edward Everett (1794–1865), 1864

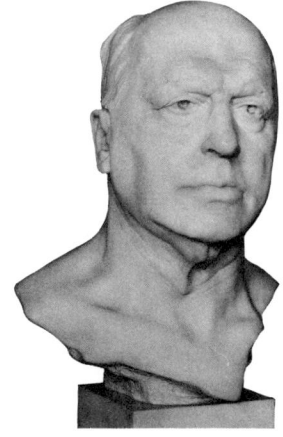

40. Capt. Francis Derwent Wood, R.A., (1872–1926), bust of Henry James, (1843–1916), 1914

42. Leopoldo Ansiglione (Italy, 1832–1899), Marble of Child and Swan

41. Left. Horatio Greenough (1805–1852), bust of Christ

43. Left, Antonio Canova (1757–1822), marble copy after, of Venus, a pendant to the copy of the Venus de Medici

44. Below. William Wetmore Story (1819–1895), Arcadian Shepherd Boy, 1855

SELECTED BIBLIOGRAPHY

Adams, Adeline Valentine (Pond). *Daniel Chester French, Sculptor.* Boston and New York, Houghton Mifflin Co. 1932.

Alexandre, Arsène. *Puvis de Chavannes.* London, George Newnes, Ltd. 1905.

Baxter, Sylvester. "John S. Sargent's Decorations for the Boston Public Library." *Harper's Weekly*, v. 39 (June 1, 1895) pp. 506–507, 509.

Baxter, Sylvester. *The Legend of the Holy Grail As Set Forth in the Frieze Painted by Edwin A. Abbey for the Boston Public Library.* Boston, Curtis and Cameron, 1904.

Benton, Josiah Henry. *The Working of the Boston Public Library;* an address by Josiah H. Benton, President of the Library Trustees, before the Beacon Society of Boston, January 2, 1909. Boston, Rockwell and Churchill Press, 1909.

Boston Public Library. *B. P. L. News*, v. 15, no. 6 (Summer, 1964). A special issue, devoted to architectural features of the Central Library.

Boston Public Library. *A Casual Tour.* Boston, Issued by the Trustees of the Boston Public Library, 1972, 1973.

Boston Public Library. *Proceedings on the Occasion of Laying the Corner-stone of the Public Library of the City of Boston,* November 28, 1888. Boston, Printed by Order of the City Council, 1889.

Boston Public Library Employees Benefit Association. *The Boston Public Library; a Handbook to the Library Building, its Mural Decorations and its Collections.* Boston, Association Press, 1939.

Boston Public Library Employees Benefit Association. *A Description of Edwin Austin Abbey's Quest of the Holy Grail.* Boston, Association Publications, 1936.

Boston Public Library Employees Benefit Association. *Handbook of the Boston Public Library.* Boston, Association Publications, 1916.

"Boston's Library." *Harper's Weekly*, v. 39 (March 2, 1895) p. 195.

Burchard, John Ely and Albert Bush-Brown. *The Architecture of America; A Social and Cultural History.* Boston, Little, Brown, 1961.

Carnegie Institute (Pittsburgh) *Catalogue of a Memorial Exhibition of the Works of Augustus Saint-Gaudens.* Pittsburgh, Carnegie Institute, 1909.

Charteris, Hon. Evan Edward. *John Sargent.* New York, Charles Scribner's Sons, 1927.

Cortissoz, Royal. "Puvis de Chavannes." *Personalities in Art.* New York, London, Charles Scribner's Sons, 1925. pp. 205–217.

Cortissoz, Royal. "Some Critical Reflections on the Architectural Genius of Charles F. McKim." *The Brickbuilder,* v. 19, no. 2 (February, 1910) pp. 23–37. Memorial issue dedicated to Charles Follen McKim.

Cox, Kenyon. *Old Masters and New; Essays in Art Criticism.* New York, Fox, Duffield and Co. 1905.

Dahl, Curtis. "English Bards and Boston Buildings." *Nineteenth Century,* v. 3, no. 1 (Spring, 1977) pp. 54–61.

Downes, William Howe. *John S. Sargent, His Life and Work.* Boston, Little, Brown and Company, 1925.

Emerson, Helen Brace. *The Holy Grail. As Depicted by E. A. Abbey in Frieze Decoration in the Boston Public Library.* Beloit, Wisconsin, Beloit College, 1904.

Fenollosa, Ernest Francisco. *Mural Painting in the Boston Public Library.* Boston, Curtis and Company, 1896.

French Symbolist Painters: Moreau, Puvis de Chavannes, Redon and their Followers. Catalogue of an Exhibition held at the Hayward Gallery, London, and the Walker Art Gallery, Liverpool, 1972. London, Arts Council, 1972.

Granger, Alfred Hoyt. *Charles Follen McKim; a Study of His Life and Work.* Boston and New York, Houghton Mifflin Company, 1913.

Greenslet, Ferris. *The Quest of the Holy Grail; An Intrepetation and a Paraphrase of the Holy Legends.* With illustrations from the frieze decoration in the Boston Public Library by Edwin Austin Abbey, R. A. Boston, Curtis and Cameron, 1902.

Hitchcock, Henry Russell. *Architecture: Nineteenth and Twentieth Centuries.* Harmondsworth, Middlesex, Penguin Books, 1958.

James, Henry. *The American Scene.* New York and London, Harper and Brothers, 1907.

Jordy, William H. *American Buildings and their Architects* (vol. 3, *Progressive and Academic Ideals at the Turn of the Twentieth Century*) Garden City, N. Y. Doubleday, 1976. Ch. VII, "The Beaux-Arts Renaissance: Charles McKim's Boston Public Library." pp. 314–375.

Lucas, Edward Verrall. *Edwin Austin Abbey, Royal Academician; the Record of His Life and Work.* London, Methuen and Company, 1921. 2 vols.

"M. Puvis de Chavannes's Panel for the Boston Public Library." *Harper's Weekly,* v. 39 (May 18, 1895) pp. 461–462.

McKibbin, David. *Sargent's Boston, with an Essay and a Biographical Summary and a Complete Check List of Sargent's Portraits.* Boston, Museum of Fine Arts, 1956. "Catalogue of a Centennial Exhibition."

McKim, Mead and White. *A Monograph of the Work of McKim, Mead and White, 1879–1915.* New York, The Architectural Book Publishing Company, 1914–1915. 4 vols.

Memorial Meeting in Honor of the Late Charles Follen McKim Held at the New Theatre, New York, November 23, 1909. New York, Privately Printed, 1909.

Moore, Charles. *The Life and Times of Charles Follen McKim.* Boston and New York, Houghton Mifflin Company, 1929.

Mount, Charles Merrill. *John Singer Sargent: a Biography.* New York, W. W. Norton, 1955.

"The New Library in Boston." *Harper's Weekly,* v. 39 (March 16, 1895) pp. 251–254.

Ormond, Richard. *John Singer Sargent: Paintings, Drawings, Watercolours.* London, Phaidon, 1970.

Price, Aimée Brown. "L'allégorie Réele Chez Pierre Puvis de Chavannes." *Gazette des Beaux Arts,* 6th Ser. v. 89 (Jan. 1977) pp. 27–40.

Richman, Michael. *Daniel Chester French, an American Sculptor.* New York, Metropolitan Museum of Art for the National Trust for Historic Preservation, 1976.

Ricketts, Charles S. "Puvis de Chavannes." *Pages on Art.* London, Constable and Company, 1913. pp. 57–79.

Saint-Gaudens, Augustus. *The Reminiscences of Augustus Saint-Gaudens.* New York, The Century Company, 1913. 2 vols.

Sisson, Thiebault. "M. Puvis de Chavannes's New Panels for the Boston Public Library." *Harper's Weekly,* v. 40 (Oct. 10, 1896) pp. 1009–1010.

Small, Herbert. *Handbook of the New Public Library in Boston.* Boston, Curtis and Company, 1895.

Smith, Preserved. "Sargent's New Mural Decorations". *Scribner's Magazine,* v. 71 (March, 1922) pp. 379–384.

Sturgis, Russell, Jr. "Bronze Doors for the Boston Public Library." *Scribner's Magazine*, v. 36 (December, 1904) pp. 765–768.

Sturgis, Russell, Jr. *The Works of McKim, Mead and White.* New York, The Architectural Record Company, 1895.

Sutton, Denys. "Elegance and Idealism." *Apollo*, vol. 105 (February, 1977) pp. 88–93. (An editorial on Daniel Chester French)

Tharp, Louise (Hall). *Saint-Gaudens and the Gilded Era.* Boston, Little, Brown, 1969.

Vachon, Marius. *Puvis de Chavannes.* Paris, Braun, Clément et Cie, 1895.

Van Dyck, Henry. "The Quest of the Holy Grail. Painted by Edwin A. Abbey for the Boston Public Library." *Harper's Weekly*, v. 39 (April 20, 1895) pp. 366–367, foldout plate, "The Siege Perilous" following p. 368.

Wadlin, Horace Greeley. *The Public Library of the City of Boston; a History.* Boston, Trustees of the Boston Public Library, 1911.

Whitehill, Walter Muir. *Boston Public Library; a Centennial History.* Cambridge, Mass. Harvard University Press, 1956.